MASTER DIGITAL TRANSFORMATION IN 7 DAYS

The Starter Guide to Business Transformation using Technology

Yoav Tchelet

Yoav Tchelet

© Copyright 2019 - All rights reserved.

It is not legal to reproduce, duplicate, or transmit any part of this document in either electronic means or in printed format. Recording of this publication is strictly prohibited and any storage of this document is not allowed unless with written permission from the publisher except for the use of brief quotations in a book review.

TABLE OF CONTENTS

Introduction

Chapter One: What Is Digital Transformation?

Chapter Two: Why Your Organization Needs Digital Transformation

Chapter Three: Elements Of Digital Transformation

Chapter Four: Aligning Staff And Company Culture To Your Digital Transformation Vision

Chapter Five: Improving Customer Experience In The Digital Age

Chapter Six: Improving Operational Processes

Chapter Seven: Challenges Of Digital Transformation

Final Words

INTRODUCTION

Digital transformation has emerged as one of the biggest trends causing disruptions within the business world. The proliferation of digital technologies has changed every aspect of our lives, from how we communicate and consume entertainment to how we shop and make payments. Seeing all these changes, businesses and organizations are also trying to see how they can take advantage of digital technologies to transform themselves and remain relevant in today's highly connected and hyper-competitive world.

Question is, where do they even start?

In this book, the author gives business owners and leaders a detailed look into digital transformation, discussing what it is, why their organizations need to adopt, and how to actually implement it within their organizations. By the end of this book, you will have a pretty good idea of what your business needs to survive and thrive in the digital age.

Ready to get started? Let's jump inside.

CHAPTER ONE: WHAT IS DIGITAL TRANSFORMATION?

Everywhere you turn nowadays, be that on the internet, in panel discussions, seminars and workshops, you will come across the message that digital transformation is imperative for any business or organization that wants to remain relevant and competitive in a world that is increasingly becoming digital. Despite this

common call for digital transformation, there is one huge problem. In most cases, a clear definition of digital transformation is not provided, which leaves most business leaders in a state of confusion as to what exactly digital transformation means and how to achieve it. Is it just another way of saying moving services and operations to the cloud? Is it the same thing as digitization? Is the organization supposed to hire a consultant to help them transform to digital?

A great deal of this confusion can be attributed to IT solutions vendors who ambiguously use and abuse the term digital transformation when marketing their solutions. Like most tech trends, the term digital transformation has become excessively hyped up and overused. So much, in fact, that the International Data Corporation (IDC) predicts that digital transformation spending will exceed $2 trillion in 2019, accounting for about 40% of all technology spending. This huge figure can be attributed to the fact that many CIOs use the term digital transformation to refer to their efforts at modernizing their organizations.

However, savvy CIOs and business leaders know that digital transformation is not a single tech solution. While tech is part of the digital transformation, there is more to it than just tech. So, what exactly is a digital transformation?

There are several definitions of digital transformation. In its most basic form, digital transformation can be defined as the process through which a business or organization creates and adopts new business and operating models that allow the business to implement, integrate and take advantage of digital, mobile, social, and other emerging technologies. The aim here is to gain new data insights that can be used to make the business more efficient and to improve the customer experience.

Digital transformation can also be defined as the process of integrating digital technologies into all areas of a business, and in so doing, changing the fundamental way in which the business operates and how it delivers value to its customers. Digital transformation involves a change in company culture that requires the organization to challenge and rethink how it uses processes, people and technology, to drive business performance.

Digital transformation requires the organization's leadership to adopt a new way of thinking that encourages experimentation and innovation, as well as the use of technology to improve the experience of the organization's clients, employees, partners, suppliers, and other key stakeholders. Sometimes, this might require the organization to do away with long-standing business processes on which the organization was built and adopt new, untested processes.

Digital transformation should start with the customer before moving on to other areas. The chief aim of digital transformation should be to provide a way for the organization to know and understand its customers better, improve the level service and deliver better customer experience. Digital transformation also requires cross-departmental collaboration. It should transcend traditional roles like marketing, sales, and customer service, and instead focus on how the whole business can work as one harmonious unit in the delivery of value and a great experience to the customer.

WHAT DIGITAL TRANSFORMATION IS NOT

Like I mentioned earlier, there is a lot of confusion about what digital transformation is not. Having explained what digital transformation is, let us take a look at what it is not.

It Is Not Just About Technology

When people first hear the term digital transformation, they automatically think about the technology aspect. However, there is more to digital transformation beyond technology. It involves coming up with new innovative solutions that drive business transformation and aligning operational processes and people to take advantage of technology to improve the business.

One of the most forgotten aspects of digital transformation is the human element, yet it is very crucial to the success of the transformation. In order for digital transformation to be effective, people need to be trained and empowered to fully utilize the technology. They have to collaborate with each other. They have to adopt a culture that promotes the use of digital technologies to improve the business. And regardless of how much an organization goes digital, non-digital interactions will also play a critical role in ensuring customer satisfaction.

It Is Not A Goal

I cannot emphasize this enough. Organizations should not treat digital transformation as a goal that they need to achieve, but rather as a new and better way of doing business. Once your business starts the digital transformation process, don't aim for a certain point where you can finally say that you have finally completed the digital transformation process. Instead, the digital transformation should be seen as an ongoing process where the organization constantly tries to come up with new ways of using digital technologies to deliver more value and better experiences to customers.

It Is Not A Single Project

Digital transformation is not defined by a single project, such as moving operations to the cloud or implementing an ERP system. Instead, it will usually involve several different projects and will continue evolving as the business grows.

DIFFERENCE BETWEEN DIGITALIZATION, DIGITIZATION, AND DIGITAL TRANSFORMATION

I also mentioned that some business leaders use the term digital transformation to refer to anything that has to do with digital technologies. Because of this, digital transformation is often confused with the terms digitalization and digitization. However, there is a difference between digital transformation and these terms.

Digitization refers to the process of moving from analog to digital. For instance, let's imagine an organization that started about two decades ago before computers became ubiquitous at the workplace. Such a business might have kept its records on paper files and used physical, printed letters for business communications. Once computers went mainstream, such a

business might have gone from keeping paper files to storing files on computers and using email for business communications. This is an example of digitization. While digitization makes it much easier to find, retrieve and share information, most business systems and processes remain largely unchanged. The only gains made here are those that are a direct result of the process of finding, retrieving and sharing information becoming faster.

Once information has been digitized, the organization can use it to make established processes much simpler and more efficient. This is what is known as digitalization. For instance, let's assume that customers used to make a call to customer reps to find out the status of their orders. With the rise of the internet and mobile technologies, it became possible for customers to check their order status through SMS or the internet whenever they wanted, even if the business was closed at the time. Note that the established way of going about this process did not change. The customer still has to make a request about their order status, which is then processed and the customer is given feedback about their order. The process only became much simpler and more efficient.

Finally, we have a digital transformation. Unlike the other two, digital transformation involves changing how you do business or coming up with an entirely new business model and adding value to every interaction a customer has with your business. A great example of a company that underwent a successful digital transformation is LEGO. After expanding rapidly, the company experienced a steady decline in sale in the 90s and was almost going bankrupt by 2004. To avoid going bankrupt, the company embarked on a digital transformation process that saw the company leverage digital technologies to come up with new sources of revenue, such as mobile games, movies and applications. This digital transformation changed the company's fortunes and it became profitable once again. In this case, digital transformation meant coming up with a new way of doing business, leveraging digital technologies to create more value for customers.

CHAPTER SUMMARY

In this chapter, you have learned:

- Digital transformation is the process through which a business adopts new business and operating models that allow the business to implement, integrate and take advantage of digital, mobile, social, and other emerging technologies.
- Digital transformation can also be defined as the integration of digital technologies into all areas of business, thus changing how the business operates and how it delivers value to customers.
- Digital transformation requires the organization's leadership to adopt a new way of thinking that encourages experimentation and innovation.
- Digital transformation should start with the customer before moving on to other areas.
- Digital transformation is not just about technology but encompasses all areas of a business.
- Digital transformation is not a goal to be achieved. It is an ongoing process where the organization constantly comes up with new ways of using digital technologies to deliver more value and better experiences to customers.
- Digital transformation is not a single project. It involves several different projects and continues evolving as the business grows.
- Digital transformation is not the same as digitization or digitalization.

In the next chapter, you will learn the benefits of digital transformation.

CHAPTER TWO: WHY YOUR ORGANIZATION NEEDS DIGITAL TRANSFORMATION

Today's business environment has become very dynamic and highly competitive. It has become for huge companies that have existed for years or decades to be by disrupted and driven out of business by smaller and more agile technology supported competitors. Many organizations undertake digital transformation in order to survive and thrive in this hyper-competitive environment. Embarking on a digital transformation journey has several benefits that help your business remain competitive and relevant.

These include:

IMPROVED EFFICIENCY

One of the greatest advantages of digital transformation is improved efficiency. As organizations move away from older ways of doing business to new, innovative processes, they eliminate the bottlenecks that may have existed in the current processes and help make the entire business more efficient. In addition, the use of technology across various aspects of the business and the use of new business models based on digital technologies also help make processes much simple and faster, thereby making the

organization more efficient.

COST REDUCTION

Optimizing business operations and using digital technologies to make processes more efficient also results in cost reductions. For instance, when Netflix went from selling movies via mail order and introduced the current model where customers simply stream the movies they want on demand, they were able to cut back on all the costs associated with mailing DVDs to customers. The cost savings of digital transformation stem from the fact that tasks can now be done much faster and more efficiently. In addition, digital transformation provides insightful data that can be used to make better decisions that result in cost savings.

IMPROVED CUSTOMER EXPERIENCE

This is perhaps the greatest benefit of digital transformation. The high penetration of technologies such as the internet, smartphones, social media, and e-commerce has created an environment where people are constantly looking for ways to make their lives easier. They want to be able to conveniently find solutions to their problems, and what's more, they want these solutions as quickly as possible. They want to be able to shop from wherever they are and to interact with your company from their smartphones.

Digital transformation offers businesses a great opportunity to meet the demands of their customers and deliver excellent customer experience. By developing multiple customer touch points supported by cutting edge digital technologies, you provide customers with a way to interact with your businesses in whatever way they want, whenever they want.

Aside from increasing the ways through which customers can interact with your business, digital transformation also makes processes much faster and more efficient, something that can be translated into improved customer experience. When customers have to wait for less to get what they want, and when their requests are handled more efficiently, the customer is likely to report a more positive experience with your business.

Finally, by creating digital touch points for customers to interact with your business, you create an awesome opportunity for your business to gather a lot of data about your customers. You can then use this data to learn more about your customers' needs and preferences and then delight them with a personalized and consistent experience regardless of the channel they are using to interact with your business.

CONSOLIDATED OPERATIONS

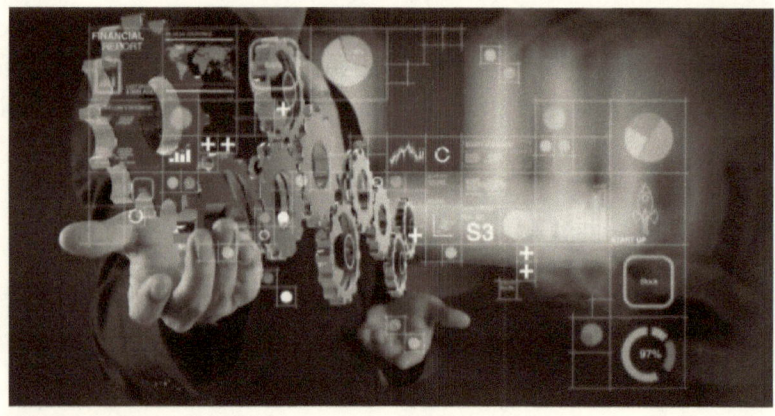

Remember, I mentioned earlier that digital transformation transcends traditional roles within the business. It brings together the entire architecture of your organization as well as your entire workforce. It incorporates agile digital systems that bring together and seamlessly integrate various aspects of your business, such as record keeping, production, decision making, project management, analytics, social media, and so on. This makes it easier for the business to achieve task automation, a collaboration of various departments in projects, better decision making, and so on. Having various aspects of your business working in harmony with each other also makes it much easier for the business to connect with customers and satisfy their needs.

EMPOWERMENT OF EMPLOYEES

Digital transformation also empowers employees by increasing their mobility and making it easier for them to share knowledge and collaborate with each other. Once work processes have been virtualized, employees can perform their tasks remotely, whether they are at home or even when they are on business trips overseas. Employees who are out in the field can also remotely access the latest information and use it to make decisions when they are out there, as well as submit their reports and findings instantly. Not only does this make employees more productive, but it also provides an opportunity for the organization to save space and increase employee satisfaction by allowing employees to work from home/remotely.

Virtualization of work processes also makes it possible for employees to collaborate with each other, even if they are not within the same physical location. For companies with a footprint across the globe, employees in one country can easily hold virtual meetings with those from a different country and gain local insights that can be very useful in the decision making process.

ANALYTICS

The use of digital technologies across various areas of the business provides an awesome opportunity for the capture and analysis of data. In business, data is very useful. The metrics of digital marketing campaigns can be monitored to determine what is working and what is not, helping the business to optimize marketing campaigns, drive revenue and decrease costs. The data can also be used to gain better insights about the needs and preferences of customers and then use these insights to deliver a more personalized and better experience to customers. Data also

provides a basis on which the organization's leadership can make better strategic decisions. All in all, the importance of data cannot be underestimated. All data provides an opportunity for the business to improve and optimize various process and increase the ROI from all the business' marketing efforts.

NEW PRODUCTS AND SERVICES

The use of digital technologies to change old ways of doing business and come up with new business models provides businesses with a great opportunity to introduce new products and services. For instance, we saw how LEGO expanded their offerings to include movies, applications and mobile games. Similarly, as part of its digital transformation agenda, Under Armour developed a fitness app that captured data about its customers' health and fitness as well as how they used its products. The company then uses this data to come up with products that are suited to

different customer segments.

ACCURATE MARKET SEGMENTATION

Using digital touch points and digital CRM systems have made it possible for businesses to maintain customer databases in a way that was previously not possible. Instead of relying on manual research to come up with customer profiles, businesses now have access to data about all customers who have bought their products. This makes it possible for businesses to segment the market and create customer profiles with unprecedented accuracy. It then becomes easier to analyze the most profitable customer segments, the segments where more marketing is needed, segments that are still untapped and so on.

CONTINUOUS IMPROVEMENT

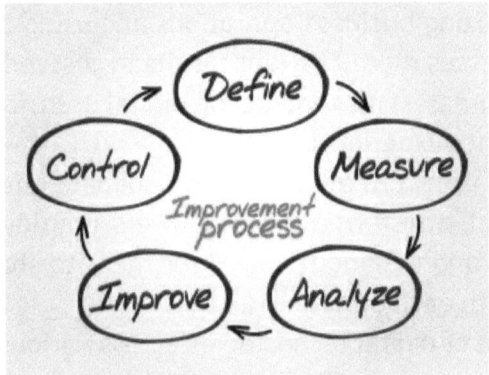

Digital transformation is an ongoing process that evolves as the business grows. Once a business embarks on its digital transformation journey, it constantly keeps evaluating what is working and what is not, identifying opportunities for making processes more efficient and finding new ways to collaborate and expand its knowledge. All these provide the business with opportunities to continuously improve and expand.

CHAPTER SUMMARY

In this chapter, you have learned:

- Digital transformation makes your business more efficient.
- Optimizing business operations and using digital technologies to make processes more efficient results in cost reductions.
- The greatest advantage of digital transformation is an improved customer experience.
- Digital transformation helps consolidate operations.
- Digital transformation empowers employees by increasing their mobility and making it easier for them to share knowledge and collaborate with each other.
- The use of digital technologies across various areas of the business provides an awesome opportunity for the capture and analysis of data.
- The use of digital technologies to change old ways of doing business and come up with new business models provides businesses with a great opportunity to introduce new products and services.
- Digital transformation makes it possible for businesses to segment the market and create customer profiles with unprecedented accuracy.
- Digital transformation is an ongoing process that evolves as the business grows.

In the next chapter, you will learn the elements of digital transformation.

CHAPTER THREE: ELEMENTS OF DIGITAL TRANSFORMATION

Digital transformation cannot be distilled down into a single project or single solution. Instead, it is a broad undertaking that encompasses several different areas. Still, digital transformation initiatives can be divided into five broad categories based on what the initiatives try to achieve. These five categories are:

CUSTOMER EXPERIENCE TRANSFORMATION

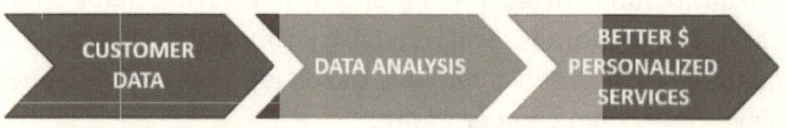

Customers are the most important people in any business, and as such, enhancing the customer experience should be at the center of any digital transformation initiatives. In order to give customers a great experience, it is important to know and understand your customers. Previously, the only way for businesses to learn about customers was through the company's CRM system, which only gave businesses limited information about the customer. With the rise of the internet and other digital platforms, however, businesses now have a great opportunity to gain a lot of insights into their customers, who they are, what their needs and motivations are, and what they expect when interacting with the business.

As customers use these new digital platforms, they leave behind a digital footprint that businesses can use to build an accurate customer profile. For instance, through social media, a business can gain geographic and demographic information about their customers as well as behavioral insights into different customers' likes and dislikes. Using data gleaned from customers' interactions with online shopping platforms, businesses can also predict customer purchasing behavior and what other products they are likely to buy based on their purchasing history. Digital platforms also give brands an opportunity to interact with their customers in a social setting and cultivate lasting relationships.

Aside from helping businesses better understand their customers, digital platforms also provide a great opportunity for marketing. Today's customers are tech-savvy and digitally connected. Before making a purchase, they often research the product on the internet and reach out to their friends on social media and other online forums to gain insights about the product before they decide to buy. In order to remain competitive, businesses need to take advantage of these digital tools for marketing. They should ensure that the business's website, social media pages, and other digital platforms provide up-to-date information about products, service promotions, and so on.

As I just mentioned above, the customer of today is tech-savvy and connected. They expect to engage and interact with businesses and organizations in a way that is most convenient for them and will be more inclined towards businesses that give them different options to interact with the business. Businesses can enhance the customer experience and remain more competitive by providing digital customer touch points that offer more convenience. For instance, a bank might launch a mobile app or an online portal where customers can perform various banking services without having to visit a physical branch. The more options customers have for conveniently interacting with a brand, the more likely the customers are to be satisfied with their experience with the brand.

Finally, businesses can also take advantage of digital technologies to transform the sales experience and drive in-person sales conversions. For instance, as part of its digital transformation initiatives, Audi built digital car showrooms where customers can virtually customize their dream audi from numerous possible configurations, experience the car

Yoav Tchelet

in life size on huge screens and even take it on a virtual test drive. Through this initiative, Audi created an unmatched user experience and was able to increase its sales conversions.

OPERATIONAL PROCESS TRANSFORMATION

While the transformation of customer experiences is the most visible and most exciting aspect of digital transformation, there are also a lot of benefits to be gained from transforming a business' operational processes. Operational process transformation is all about making processes more efficient and saving time and money. Operational process transformation involves three key initiatives, which are:

Process Digitization

This involves converting manual processes into digital and possibly automated processes in order to save time, reduce costs or make the processes more productive. By automating manual processes, employees are freed up so that they can refocus their attention on creativity, innovation, and strategy, rather than repetitive tasks. Automation also makes the business more responsive to changes and more scalable, which is critical for any business that wants to remain competitive in today's highly dynamic business environment. In addition, digitization and automation of processes create streams of data that can be exploited to make processes even more efficient. For instance, IOT sensors can be used to track inventory in warehouses or track deliveries, not only making these processes more efficient but also providing data which can be mined to provide better insights into how these processes can be made more efficient.

Process digitization also involves taking advantage of the SMAC stack to improve business processes. SMAC stands for social, mobile, analytics and cloud. By taking advantage of social platforms, businesses can enhance how they interact and communicate with customers. By taking advantage of mobile technologies, processes can be freed from the physical location, such that employees can still do their work regardless of where they are, at any time and on any device. Using big data analytics and artificial intelligence, the data streams created by digitization of process can be turned into insights that can be used to optimize processes and make more robust decisions. Finally, a business can also take advantage of cloud technologies to create uniform business processing platforms.

Worker Enablement

Worker enablement involves the use of digital technologies to create an environment that enhances collaboration between workers and makes their work easier. We have already seen how digital technologies can be used to virtualize work and eliminate the locational constraints of work. For instance, using mobile platforms, workers out in the field can update their reports and findings immediately, without having to physically visit the office.

Digital technologies can also be used to allow workers to easily collaborate, even if they are not within the same physical location. Employees in different cities or countries can easily talk with and share information and knowledge using tools such as virtual conferencing technologies, screen sharing and file collaboration tools, online team collaboration and project management tools such as slack and asana, and so on. All these technologies give more power to employees and make business processes much faster and more efficient.

Performance Management

Operational process transformation also involves the use of digital systems to track and manage performance. Digital systems provide business leaders with deeper insights into the performance of different products, customer segments and regions, allowing them to make decisions based on real data rather than estimates and assumptions. This kind of performance tracking and management can be applied to both internal and customer-facing business processes.

BUSINESS MODEL TRANSFORMATION

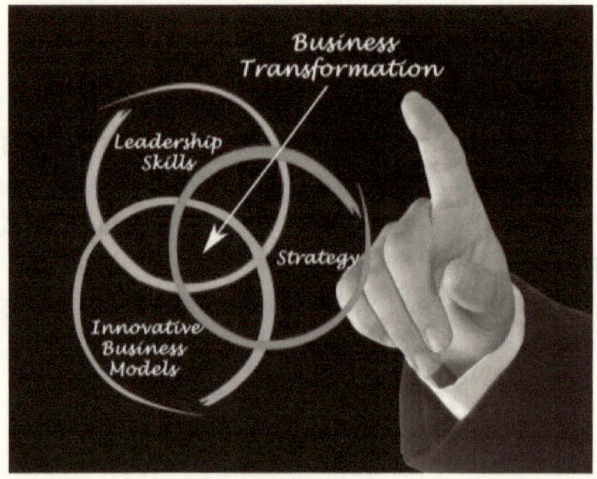

In many cases, digital transformation involves more than improving the customer experience or transforming business processes. Sometimes, the digital transformation might call for a redefinition of the entire business model. Business model transformation usually involves two major approaches:

Digitally Modifying The Business

In today's business environment where almost every

customer is online, businesses that fail to flexibly adapt to online and digital strategies are on their deathbed. Digital transformation involves modifying your business model in order to meet your customers

Digital Transformation

where they are – within the digital space.

One of the best examples of companies that have been able to digitally modify their business model is Netflix. When the company started in 1997, it's a business model was offering DVD rentals by mail. When the company realized that more and more people were consuming media online, the company modified its business model to online movie streaming in 2007 while retaining its DVD rentals by mail service.

Another good example of a company that digitally modified its business is The New York Times. Two decades ago, it was a common sight to find people's noses buried in newspapers during the morning commute. The rise of digital publishing, however, changed the game and newspaper sales across the country fell from about $60 billion to about $20 billion between the year 2000 and 2015, according to the Atlantic. To avoid feeling this pinch, the New York Times shifted to a new model where they delivered news over digital platforms on a subscription model. Whereas other newspaper companies were experiencing decreased sales, the New York Times continued experiencing growth. In 2017, the New York Times brought in about $500 million in digital revenue, according to their annual report.

Therefore, as part of its digital transformation efforts, your business should find ways of augmenting its traditional business model with digital offerings.

Creating New Digital Businesses

Aside from finding a way to modify and augment existing business models using technology, businesses can also transform their business model by introducing totally new digital products and services. We already looked at the example of how LEGO, as part of their digital transformation efforts, introduced new digital products – movies, applications, and mobile games – which were not part of their initial offerings.

Another great example of a business model transformation can be found in the approach being taken by the gym industry. Traditionally, gyms earn money by charging customers a subscription to access the facility and use the equipment. However, to take advantage of digital, many gyms and gym instructors have added a new business model where they create training regimens for people trying to achieve certain results and then sell these regimens either through websites or mobile apps.

CHAPTER SUMMARY

In this chapter, you have learned:

- Enhancing the customer experience should be at the center of any digital transformation initiatives.

- The second element of digital transformation is the transformation and optimization of operational processes.

- The third element of digital transformation is the transformation of an organization's business model so that organizations can meet their customers where they are – within the digital space.

In the next chapter, you will learn how to align your staff and corporate culture to your digital transformation vision.

CHAPTER FOUR: ALIGNING STAFF AND COMPANY CULTURE TO YOUR DIGITAL TRANSFORMATION VISION

One of the most forgotten aspects in most digital transformation initiatives is the people and cultural aspect. In order to achieve a successful digital transformation, there is a need for a company culture that is conducive to the change. Any business or organization can introduce new technologies and propose changes to processes and infrastructure. However, without addressing the human element and bringing your staff on board in the changes, it is next to impossible to achieve lasting change. The people will soon go back to using the old ways, making your attempts at digital transformation ineffective.

Not sold yet? Below are some reasons why you should pay more attention to company culture when implementing your digital transformation strategy:

- Not everyone within the organization will understand why the organization is adopting new tools and processes or how the benefits these tools and processes will bring to the organization. Therefore, some managers might continue supporting the old way of doing things in tandem with the new processes, not only creating confusion but also resulting in a lot of repetitive work that will negatively impact productivity.

- People don't like change. If people have been using a particular system or following a particular process for decades, they won't be too enthusiastic about the change. Therefore, some of your staff might continue following the old way of doing things, not because the old way is more effective, but because that is what they are used to.
- Sometimes, implementing a digital transformation strategy might require other parties within your value chain or distribution network – some of whom you have no control over – to make changes to adapt to your new way of doing things. Without selling your vision to these key stakeholders and training them on the new ways of working, they might not be keen on making the required changes, which will make your digital transformation efforts ineffective.

In a survey of 40 digital transformation case studies, the Boston Consulting Group, a global management consulting firm, found that only 17% of companies that ignored company culture while undergoing their digital transformation were able to achieve any improvements in financial performance. On the other hand, 90% of companies that paid attention to and fostered a digital culture saw significant improvements in financial performance.

What this shows is that as a business leader, you cannot assume that your staff will embrace the transformation simply because you have ordered them to do so. Therefore, before you embark on your digital transformation journey, you must actively take steps to align your staff and company culture to your digital transformation vision. Question is, how do you do this?

Yoav Tchelet

The next few pages include some tips on how to bring your staff on board with your vision and strategy.

SHARE YOUR VISION

One of the greatest mistakes most business leaders make with their digital transformation is to take a top-down approach, where the management makes a decision which must then be implemented by lower levels of the organization simply because it came from top management. The problem with this approach is that there is no staff buy-in, and most organizations that take this approach do not succeed.

Therefore, what you want to do first is to share your vision with your employees and make sure that the entire organization knows the direction it is headed and why. Before you start implementing the changes, explain to your staff why you are implementing these changes, what you aim to achieve by implementing them, and how the changes are aligned with the organization's overall vision. What customer experience goals do you want to achieve? What operational processes do you want to improve? How will the proposed changes impact employee experience?

Explaining your vision and answering the above questions should be the first step before you even start creating a strategy that will drive your digital transformation. Not only does this make it clear to employees why the changes are necessary, but it also gives you the opportunity to work with your employees to create a strategy, therefore making them more invested in the transformation.

ADOPT RELEVANT TECHNOLOGY

Many organizations assume that digital transformation is all about technology, and so they go out and procure every new technology that they can lay their hands on. Unfortunately, this is not the way to achieve digital transformation. If anything, this shows that your organization does not know what it is doing. This will, in turn, result in your staff undermining the technology and the entire process in general, because they would find the process irrelevant.

Instead, what you need to do is to make sure that all the new technology you adopt is relevant. Having answered questions about what you want to achieve with your digital transformation initiative, go for technologies that will make it possible for you to achieve those goals. This not only does this make your efforts more efficient, it also makes your staff more committed to the change, since they can actually see how the technology and process changes are driving the organization closer to its goals, rather than having new technology and new processes dumped on them for technology's sake, without aiding the achievement of goals in any way.

TRAIN YOUR STAFF ON NEW PROCESSES AND TECHNOLOGIES

One of the greatest sources of employee resistance when it comes to digital transformation is the lack of digital skills. If your employees are not conversant with new digital tools, you cannot expect them to be enthusiastic about transitioning from their trusted ways of doing things to the new ways. Therefore, you should make building your employees' digital skills a key priority. You need to conduct an assessment of the gaps that exist between current expertise and capabilities and the needs that will arise once your company undergoes the transformation, and then invest resources to close these gaps.

There are many approaches to building your employees' digital skills, including hiring coaches to train your staff, offering employees a stipend to take digital skills courses, developing an eLearning class for your staff, using interactive training methods, peer-assisted learning, and so on.

For instance, when undergoing its digital transformation, cosmetics company L'Oreal realized that its employees did not have the skills required to make the transition to a digital way of doing business. To build its staff's capacity, L'Oreal partnered with a leading digital training specialist and built a digital marketing eLearning program. All of the company's marketing employees went through the program, and as a result, the company has become a force to reckon with in the digital marketing space.

ALLOW YOUR STAFF TO DECIDE AND CHOOSE

Many business leaders are of the view that giving staff the freedom to decide and choose is a recipe for chaos and disaster. However, the opposite is true. When staff is given the freedom to make their own decisions, they become creative and start coming up with innovative ways of improving and streamlining processes. Therefore, when you start implementing your digital transformation initiatives, don't try to exert too much control over your employees. Instead, give them the freedom to take the new

technologies and processes and run with them. Doing this makes them feel empowered, which will make them more invested in the trans-

Yoav Tchelet

formation. In addition, since they are the ones who will be primarily using these technologies and processes, they are better placed to recognizing all the new and exciting possibilities.

BE OPEN TO SUGGESTIONS

This is closely related to the previous point. If you want your digital transformation efforts to be successful, you cannot afford to be rigid or closed-minded. Remember, while technology is an important part of the digital transformation, it does not actually bring the transformation by itself. Rather, it only facilitates the transformation. Therefore, once you implement technology and process changes, you should not stop at that. Instead, you want to create a robust feedback mechanism to capture the opinions and views of your staff in regards to the technology. Use whatever information and suggestions they provide to improve and optimize the entire process. Considering they are the ones who are using these technologies directly, you cannot afford to not listen to them.

As I close this chapter, I want to reiterate one key thing. Digital transformation is more than adopting new tech tools or changing processes. If you want your digital transformation initiative to be successful, you should put your staff at the forefront of the transformation. Be transparent with them and give them the freedom to make decisions, choose and innovate, and you will definitely see the transformation you want.

CHAPTER SUMMARY

In this chapter, you have learned:

- In order to achieve successful digital transformation, there is a need for a company culture that is conducive to the change.
- Without addressing the human element and bringing your staff on board in the changes, it is next to impossible to achieve lasting change.
- You should start by sharing your vision with your employees and make sure that the entire organization knows the direction it is headed and why.
- You should make sure that all the new technology you adopt is relevant. Don't adopt new technology just for the sake of it.
- Building your employees' digital skills should be a key priority.
- When you start implementing digital transformation initiatives, don't exert too much control over your employees. Instead, give them the freedom to take the new technologies and processes and run with them.
- Create a robust feedback mechanism to capture the opinions and views of your staff in regards to the technology.

In the next chapter, you will learn how to improve customer experience in the digital age.

CHAPTER FIVE: IMPROVING CUSTOMER EXPERIENCE IN THE DIGITAL AGE

In chapter two, I mentioned that one of the major aims of digital transformation is to improve customer experience, and I will tell you why this is so important. Digital technologies have had a very huge impact on consumer habits. The rise of e-commerce, mobile devices and apps, automation, and other similar technologies has created an on-demand economy where customers want immediate access to goods, services, and brands. This new economy is not driven by businesses, but rather by consumers. They are constantly connected, they are digital natives and have a clear idea of what they can achieve with technology.

With this new breed of consumers, businesses cannot afford to skimp when it comes to offering a flawless customer experience. It is no longer an added advantage, but rather an essential that has the power to make or break your business. Considering that most of today's customer's first interaction with brands is through a digital platform, your business needs to take advantage of digital technology to provide an excellent customer experience, else these customers will quickly move on to competitors who are easily within reach. Below, we take a look at how you can improve customer experience in the age of the connected, digital native consumer.

KNOW THE WHY BEHIND EACH WHY

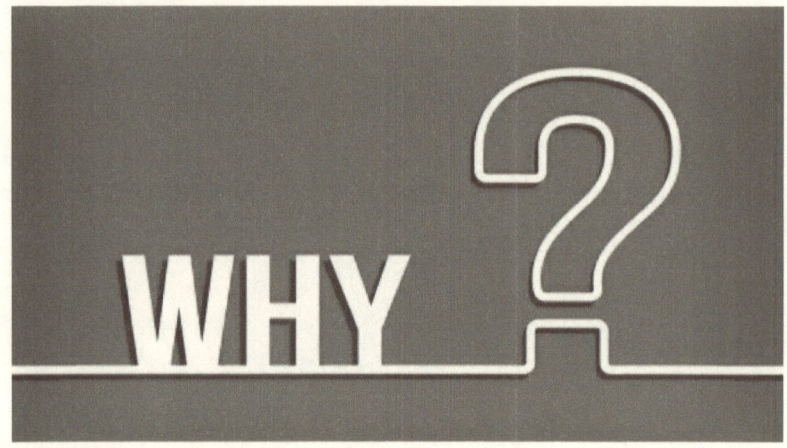

Creating an excellent customer experience is all about building customer interactions that meet and exceed the expectations of the customer. In order to do this, you need to have a very deep understanding of your customers and what they want. What I mean by knowing the why behind each why is that you should go behind the obvious reason a customer wants a certain thing or complains about something and deal with the underlying pain point.

For instance, let's assume that you are a software company who just noticed that a lot of customers are complaining that your customer service reps are taking a lot of time before responding to customer requests. Once you investigate the issue with your customer service reps, you find out that an increase in sales has resulted in more customers getting in touch with customer service reps to help them solve issues arising during the installation or use of the product.

On the surface, the problem seems to be an overwhelmed customer service department, and some organizations might respond to this situation by increasing the number of customer service reps. However, savvy business leaders will look at the underlying problem. Customers are complaining about the response time, but that is not their main pain point. If the customers didn't have issues installing or using the product, they wouldn't need to talk to customer service, and the customer service wouldn't be overwhelmed. Therefore, the problem is not the response time, but rather the challenges in using the software. Instead of increasing the number of customer service reps, a savvy business leader will use tools such as video tutorials, step by step guides or a comprehensive FAQs section on their website to ensure that customers do not have trouble installing or using the product.

Similarly, before you make any step towards improving the customer experience, you should find out your customer's real pain points rather than the symptoms, and then try to come up with ways to address these pain points. To find out the actual pain points, you can use all the tools within your disposal. Analyze any data you have about your customers, talk to your customers, conduct surveys, and so on. The point here is to have a very clear idea about your customers, their likes and dislikes, their motivations, their expectations, and so on.

PROVIDE A MULTI-CHANNEL EXPERIENCE

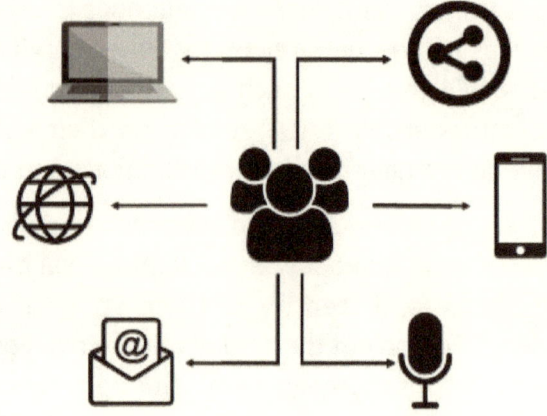

Digital channels have provided consumers with a plethora of options when it comes to interacting with businesses and finding the products or services they are looking for. They use Google to find products and services, use social media, online forums, and review sites to find out more about these products, shop for products through online shops and mobile applications, and use social media to reach out to your support team. Therefore, if you are still stuck up on just a physical store and a phone-based contact center, you are missing out on a lot of customers.

If you want to improve customer experiences through digital transformation, you should start taking advantage of digital platforms to interact with and engage your customers. However, don't just stick to

Digital Transformation

one platform. Provide your customers with multiple channels for interacting with your business. For instance, when it comes to customer support, give your customers the option of contacting your support team via phone call, email, chat or social media. When it comes to online shopping, you can provide your customers with the option of browsing and ordering products via the web or mobile app.

When using multiple channels, ensure that there is seamless integration between the different channels such that customers can switch from one channel to the next without having to start all over again or repeat themselves. For instance, if a customer was browsing products on your website and added some items to their cart, they should be able to continue with their shopping process on the mobile app where they left, without having to re-add the items to the cart again. This will contribute to the improved customer experience.

While it is important to deliver a multi-channel web experience, I will give one disclaimer. Don't add a channel just for the sake of it. For instance, some businesses might create handles and pages on multiple social media platforms but remain active on only one or two of these platforms. Let's say your business has profiles on Facebook, Twitter, Instagram, and Pinterest, but is only active on Facebook and Instagram. Any customers who try interacting with your business on Twitter or Pinterest will feel ignored, thereby negatively impacting their experience with your company. If you have no intention of actively operating a channel, it is best to avoid it completely. To avoid running yourself thin, the best

 approach is to find the channels most preferred by your customers and then focus your efforts on these.

MAKE INFORMATION AVAILABLE ONLINE

Instead of simply storing information pertaining to customers online, why not store it on the cloud? This not only makes your data safer, but it also allows you to give your customers the option of using online tools to access information. This is an easier, more reliable and convenient way for your customers to access information compared to having to send queries to a customer support representative and having to wait for hours to get the information.

A good example of companies that are doing this correctly is Amazon and other online retailers. These retailers put all the information pertaining to customer purchases online, such that a customer can simply log in onto the website and check their current and previous orders, track deliveries, cancel orders or return an order, all these without having to talk to a customer service agent. This greatly enhances the customer experience and makes the customer more comfortable interacting with and purchasing from your business.

TAKE ADVANTAGE OF AI

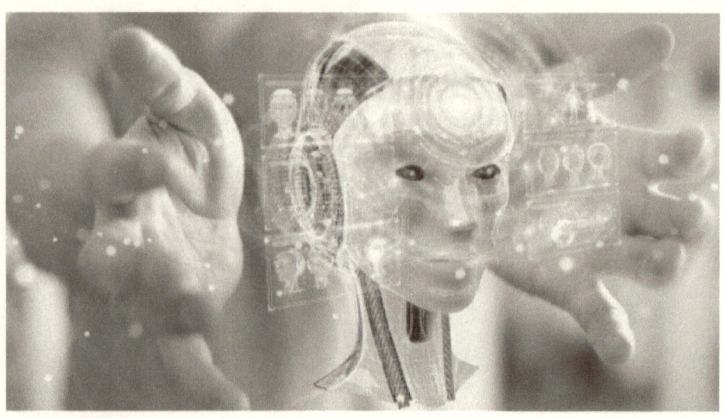

Artificial intelligence is a technology that has come up as a major driving force in the revolution of business using technology. Combined with machine learning and data analytics, artificial intelligence provides businesses with endless possibilities for improving the customer experience. The benefits of artificial intelligence stem from its excellent capabilities when it comes to detecting patterns. Using AI tools, businesses can analyze data about past customer behavior and get good insights about what problems customers are facing and the patterns in the occurrence of these problems.

Using predictive analytics, businesses can then foresee and avert these problems before they even occur, thereby helping ensure a more satisfying customer experience. Aside from detecting and preventing customer problems before they occur, AI tools can also be used to predict consumer needs and trends and come up with offers and other innovative solutions at the right time, thereby enriching the customer experience even further.

Finally, AI offers businesses the chance to treat customers as individuals and give them personalized service. For instance, businesses using AI enabled customer management systems can identify and address each customer by their name, understand and empathize by the personal choices of each individual customer, and recommend products based on the customer's personality and past purchases. For instance, streaming sites like YouTube and Netflix have algorithms that recommend videos and movies a person might like based on what they have watched previously. This can greatly enhance the customer experience.

When it comes to AI systems and data, I want to make one disclaimer. As part of delivering great customer experience, you should be very transparent with the data you collect from customers. The customers of today are tech savvy and they know businesses are collecting their data. Still, they want the ability to review and control what businesses can do with this data. Therefore, don't try to hide the fact that you are collecting their data. Be transparent about what kind of information you are collecting and how you intend to use it.

EMBRACE AUTOMATION

Automation is another great way of offering a great customer experience because it ensures quick service. Being constantly connected, today's customers might interact with a business at any time and from anywhere in the world, and they expect a quick response around the clock. If they don't get a quick response, they won't hesitate to move on to your competitors. Automation offers you a way to get around this without losing your customers.

With automation, you can have applications and bots that provide customers with feedback to their queries around the clock. Aside from applications and bots, automating tasks such as follow up emails and customer tickets can also make your customer experience more satisfying. For instance, using services such as Aweber and MailChimp, you can set up emails that are automatically sent to customers based on the customer's action on your website, thus enhancing their experience interacting with your business without the need to have personnel driving the interaction.

And if you are tempted to think that the human touch makes for better customer experience, you might be in for a rude shock. While automation was associated with a poor quality of service during its early days, it has gotten to a point where customers actually prefer automated interactions. In a survey conducted by Accenture, 84% of those surveyed reported that they preferred automated interactions to human interactions because automated applications are available around the clock.

68% of those surveyed also reported said that they preferred automated applications because they provide faster engagements compared to humans, while 64% said they found automated applications to be more polite compared to humans. Therefore, if you hadn't started using automation to enhance your customer experience, it is about time you got started.

FOCUS ON PROVIDING VALUE

 While it is important to use digital technologies to enhance the customer experience, your focus should always be on providing value. Before building an app or embracing a certain platform, you should have a clear idea of how it will contribute towards improving your customer experience. Never adopt new technology or a new platform just for the sake of it. Instead, put more effort into identifying areas where your customers might be experiencing some dissatisfaction and then determine how you can use technology to improve these areas.

CHAPTER SUMMARY

In this chapter, you have learned:

- Creating an excellent customer experience is all about building customer interactions that meet and exceed the expectations of the customer.
- You should go behind the obvious reason a customer wants a certain thing or complains about something and deal with the underlying pain point.
- When it comes to the provision of digital platforms for your customers to interact with and engage your business, don't stick to one platform. Provide them with multiple options.
- Give customers the option of accessing information and managing their orders online.
- Take advantage of AI to learn customer behavior patterns, predict customer behavior and give customers personalized service.
- With automation, you can provide customers with feedback to their queries around the clock.
- While it is important to use digital technologies to enhance the customer experience, your focus should always be on providing value.

In the next chapter, you will learn how to improve operational processes through digital transformation.

CHAPTER SIX: IMPROVING OPERATIONAL PROCESSES

Business leaders have always known that constantly improving operational processes to improve quality and efficiency and reduce costs is a key aspect of maintaining a competitive advantage. During the industrial revolution, companies and organizations improved operational processes through industrial innovations. For instance, in 1913, Henry Ford introduced the moving assembly line and reduced the manufacturing time of the Model T from 12 hours to about 2 hours, thereby making the automobile cheap enough for the masses.

Currently, the world is undergoing the digital revolution, and instead of relying on industrial innovations, businesses are now using digital technologies, such as process automation, artificial intelligence, machine learning, and intelligent information management, to make business processes more efficient and improve productivity. In this chapter, we take a look at the key things you need to keep in mind when improving your business processes using digital technologies.

START BY ASSESSING CURRENT PROCESSES

One thing I have noticed during my career as a digital transformation consultant is that very often, business leaders are convinced to embrace digital ways of doing things by marketers trying to sell them one tech solution or the other. The problem with this approach is that many business leaders end up adopting tech not because it brings any significant benefits, but simply so that they can say their organizations are digital. Not only is this costly, but it is also inefficient.

To make sure that their business process improvement initiatives are efficient and avoid wasting money, business leaders should start by conducting an audit of all their current business processes, with the aim of identifying any inefficiencies that might exist. Once you identify inefficiencies, you should then start figuring out how you can use technology to eliminate these inconsistencies. Some of the areas and processes that technology might help make more efficient may include:

- Capturing customer data in a simple and efficient way.
- Storage, management, retrieval and sharing of information.
- Eliminating duplication and minimizing repetitive tasks.
- Addressing obstacles that might be making some task more expensive or more time-consuming.

DEVELOPMENT SHOULD BE LED BY PROCESS OWNERS

While the IT team and other technical experts are a crucial element when it comes to using digital technologies to improve operational processes, it is good to keep in mind that they are only facilitators. The main focus of the improvement should be the process owners, the people who use these processes every single day. Therefore, the IT team should not develop solutions in isolation. They should be in constant consultation with the process owners. Since they interact with these processes on a daily basis, the process owners, they have a better idea of the solutions that will better solve the inefficiencies they face. The process owners are also more likely to embrace the change more readily when they are involved in the design process, and they will be invested in ensuring the success of the transformation initiatives.

Aside from the process owners, any other stakeholders who will be affected by the change should be made part of the digital transformation initiative. These include people such as suppliers, customers, resellers, and any other people who are directly or indirectly dependent on the process.

TAKE ADVANTAGE OF DEVOPS AND THE CLOUD TO MODERNIZE INFRASTRUCTURE

One of the greatest impediments to digital transformation is legacy infrastructure. In order for any company to undergo digital transformation and improve its operational processes, it has to modernize its infrastructure. One of the best ways to do this is to move processes to the cloud. Moving to the cloud has several benefits. It is a lot cheaper because there is no need to overhaul the entire system. The cloud also makes it easier to scale up or down based on demand without. Moving to the cloud is also easier to implement and enhances collaboration among workers. Taking advantage of DevOps can also allow your IT team to develop, test and implement solutions a lot more easily.

OPTIMIZE OPERATIONS WITH DATA AND ARTIFICIAL INTELLIGENCE

While technology has always been at the forefront of improving operational processes, the amount of data being produced today and the rise of artificial intelligence systems to analyze and interpret this data has made it possible for organizations to improve operations to previously unimagined levels. If digital technologies are the backbone of your operational processes, there is already a lot of data that is being generated every time you run these processes, although you might not be putting this data to maximum use. The key is to combine this data with AI systems that can analyze the data, identify patterns, and give you insights on areas where there are inefficiencies and bottlenecks, and how these bottlenecks and inefficiencies can be eliminated.

GO FOR SOLUTIONS THAT ALLOW AGILITY

Today's business conditions and environment are very dynamic, and as technology continues advancing, you can bet that this is not about to change any time soon. Therefore, even as you look for technologies to improve your operational processes, go for solutions that will allow your business to quickly react to changing conditions and new opportunities. If you go for complex and cumbersome deployments, not only will it take you lots of time to implement them, but you will be soon encumbered with inefficient systems after the business conditions change, as they will inevitably do.

SAVE TIME THROUGH AUTOMATION

As you audit your current operational processes, did you identify any tasks and processes that can be automated using technology? These are the processes that are done over and over again without any major changes in how they are done. If there are such processes, you can automate them and free up your staff to work on other tasks.

For instance, while hiring is a very critical task in every organization, it can be time-consuming. It can take your HR department weeks to go through hundreds of applications. Instead of wasting all these precious man hours, you can automate the process using an applicant tracking system (ATS), which can read through all the applications and provide you with a filtered list of the most eligible candidates within a few minutes or hours.

DEFINE KPI METRICS

Once you embark on your digital transformation journey, you want to make sure that your efforts are actually working. To be able to do this, you will need to define the Key Performance Indicator (KPI) metrics that you will track to monitor how effective your digitization efforts are. Examples of metrics that can help you determine the effectiveness of your digitization efforts include customer satisfaction ratings, cost savings, time savings, productivity, and so on.

While monitoring KPI metrics to measure effectiveness is good, don't stop at that. You should use these metrics to continually optimize and improve your operational process. Remember, operational excellence is not a destination, it is a journey. Therefore, as your business continues evolving and growing, and as the needs of your customers, employees and other stakeholders keep changing, you will need to keep monitoring these key metrics and finding opportunities for improvement.

CHAPTER SUMMARY

In this chapter, you have learned:

- Business leaders should start by conducting an audit of all their current business processes, with the aim of identifying any inefficiencies that might exist.
- The IT team should develop solutions in consultation with the process owners.
- In order for any company to undergo digital transformation and improve its operational processes, it has to modernize its infrastructure.
- By combining data and artificial intelligence, your business can uncover numerous opportunities for optimizing operations.
- Even as businesses look for technologies to improve operational processes, they should go for solutions that will allow them to quickly react to changing conditions and new opportunities.
- Automation of repetitive tasks can save time and free up employees to work on other tasks.
- Businesses need to define KPI metrics that they will track to monitor how effective digitization efforts are.

In the next chapter, you will learn some of the challenges of digital transformation.

CHAPTER SEVEN: CHALLENGES OF DIGITAL TRANSFORMATION

While digital transformation is a crucial process if you want your business to remain relevant and competitive in today's dynamic and highly connected business environment, it is not an easy journey. As you seek to transform your business or organization, you will face many challenges which you have to overcome your initiative to be successful. In this chapter, we take a look at some of the common challenges you are likely to encounter as you transform your business.

EMPLOYEE PUSHBACK

By nature, humans do not love change. Once we get used to a routine or a certain way of doing things, we become comfortable and come to trust that way of doing things. This is an evolutionary trait that made it easier for humans to survive. Once you are used to a certain way of doing things, you expend less mental energy doing it since you know what to expect. In some cases, you can even do it on autopilot. Changing from routine means you have to learn new things and deal with all the unknowns that come with the new way of doing things.

With this natural human aversion to change, you can bet that your employees are not going to take enthusiastically to the proposed changes. To them, change means uncertainty. It challenges their skills and their role within the organization, and in some cases, it could even mean the loss of their jobs. Therefore, employees will often try to push back against change to avoid the uncertainty that change brings.

Employee pushback can manifest itself in a number of ways. The finance department might derail the funding of the digital transformation project, there might be claims that the project will take away resources from other key projects, the project might even be taken through a very rigorous approval process meant to ensure that it doesn't get approved, or there might even be claims that it will negatively impact other sources of revenue. For instance, way before digital cameras took over the market, Kodak had already invented the digital camera. However, the project was shelved due to concerns that the digital camera would cannibalize the film business.

While change is risky and uncertain, it is necessary if your business is to remain relevant and competitive. Therefore, you have to find a way to overcome employee resistance to digital transformation. The best way to minimize and eliminate employee pushback is to involve your employees in the entire process. Be transparent with them, let them know why the process is important, what the organization is trying to achieve, how it will impact employee experience and what is at stake if the organization does not transform. This will make them more invested in the project and more likely to embrace it.

LACK OF CLEAR VISION AND STRATEGY

You might be surprised to learn that majority, of businesses, do not have any long term plan on how they will implement digital transformation. They simply adopt new tech tools and create some cool experiences for the customer in a piece-meal fashion. According to a report by Capgemini Consulting and MIT, only 17% of companies have a corporate-wide strategy in place for their digital transformation. With such a low figure, it is no wonder that many companies do not see any success in their efforts. After all, you cannot hit your target if you have no target in the first place. While a vision and strategy won't bring success by itself, it gives you a sense of direction and a guideline for what you are trying to achieve.

With this in mind, the first step for any company that wants to undergo digital transformation should be to come up with a vision of what it wants to achieve and then create a plan on how to achieve this vision. Study your customers and understand their unmet needs, motivations and expectations, find out what operational processes are inefficient, study what competitors are doing, and so on. With the information gained at this point, come up with a vision of how you want your organization to be within a certain time frame.

Once that is done, determine what you need to do to achieve this vision and the technological tools necessary to take you there. Define the roles each one will play towards the achievement of this vision, create project milestones and timelines, and create a budget for the project. You should also ensure that departments are following the same roadmap to avoid mis-aligned priorities. Finally, remember that digital transformation is a continuous undertaking, so you should think long term when formulating your strategy.

INEFFECTIVE COLLECTION AND USE OF CUSTOMER DATA

Customer data is one of the key anchors of a successful digital transformation initiative. In order to provide a great customer experience, you need to access data which will help you gain insights on how to enhance the customer experience. This is where a lot of companies fail. Either they don't collect the right data or they have a siloed approach to data collection, resulting in scattered scraps, without any clear way of bringing the data together. Yet some companies may have the right customer data, but may not have figured out the best way of using this data.

The solution to this challenge is to start by determining the kind of data that would help your business provide a better experience and sell more effectively. Once you identify what constitutes the right data, figure out the best way to collect this data and store it in such a way that it can be easily accessed and retrieved. Finally, use the help of AI systems and other data analysis tools to make sense of the data and see how you can take advantage of it to sell more effectively and provide a better experience to your customers.

BUDGET LIMITATIONS

In as much as it would be nice to be able to do anything you wanted without worrying about finances, the truth is that budgetary constraints are very real, and your company most likely does not have a bottomless pool of money. As part of your digital transformation initiative, you will need to build or adopt new tech solutions, train your employees, and so on. All this might need substantial investment, and justifying this extra spend might be quite a challenge. If you have budgetary constraints, the best approach is to start small. Rather than trying to do everything at once, build a strategy that allows you to implement your digital transformation initiatives in phases that your budget can allow, even if it takes several years to complete the implementation.

BEING STUCK UP ON YOUR OLD BUSINESS MODEL

Lastly, some businesses and organizations are unable to achieve successful digital transformation because they are too stuck up on legacy business models. They only see digital- transformation as the provision of the same products and services through a digital medium. While this approach is also valid, it does not always work. Sometimes, undergoing a successful digital transformation will require your organization to shift to an entirely new business model. You might have to freely provide a service that you used to charge for, come up with new products that you had never previously considered, find new, unconventional ways of monetizing your products, and so on.

If you want your digital transformation initiatives to be successful, you must be flexible and move with the times, rather than remain stuck up in legacy business models that might become obsolete at any minute. Of course, in order to let go of old business models and adopt new, unconventional models, you must be willing to experiment and take risks.

CHAPTER SUMMARY

In this chapter, you have learned:

- Humans have a natural aversion to change, and your employees are not going to take enthusiastically to changes. The best way to minimize employee pushback is to involve them in the entire process.

- The first step for any company that wants to undergo digital transformation should be to come up with a vision of what it wants to achieve and then create a plan on how to achieve this vision.

- Many companies do not effectively collect and use customer data. The solution is to determine the right kind of data to collect, figure out the best way to collect and store the data, and finally use AI systems and data analysis tools to see how they can take advantage of the data.

- If you have budgetary constraints, the best approach is to start small and build a strategy that allows you to implement your digital transformation initiatives in phases that your budget can allow.

- Companies that want to achieve successful digital transformation must be flexible and willing to experiment and take risks, rather than remaining stuck up in legacy business.

FINAL WORDS

Thank you for sticking with me to the end of this book.

Digital transformation is taking the business world by storm, and this is with good reason. Digital technologies have taken over and transformed every aspect of our daily lives, and in so doing, they have also transformed consumer habits and expectations. The customers of today are highly connected and expect to interact with businesses the same way they do in other aspects of their lives – through digital channels. Therefore, any business that wants to survive in this digital and highly connected world needs to have a digital strategy.

The good thing is, this book has provided you with the basics you need to guide your business or organization through a digital transformation. You now know what digital transformation is, the benefits it brings to your business, the elements of digital transformation, how to align your staff and company culture to your digital transformation vision, how to improve customer experience in the digital age, how to improve operational processes through digital technologies, and how to overcome the challenges you might encounter on your digital transformation journey. All that is left for you now is to go out and start crafting a digital strategy for your business.

Before you go, I have one request. If you loved this book, I want to request you to leave your honest review of the book on Amazon. I will greatly appreciate your feedback.

www.ingramcontent.com/pod-product-compliance
Lightning Source LLC
Chambersburg PA
CBHW031925170526
45157CB00008B/3054